CAVAFY GONE

Cavafy gone Gothic

BRIAN EARNSHAW

 redcliffe

First published in 2008 by Redcliffe Press Ltd.,
81g Pembroke Road, Bristol BS8 3EA

www.redcliffepress.co.uk

© Brian Earnshaw

ISBN 978 1 906593 06 3

British Library Cataloguing-in-Publication-Data
A catalogue record for this book is available from the British
Library

Cover designed by Stephen Morris, the book typeset by
Harper Phototypesetters Ltd., Northampton, and printed by
4edge Limited, Hockley. www.4edge.co.uk

Contents

Explanation

It is unlikely that the Egyptian Greek poet and native of Alexandria, Constantine Cavafy (1863–1933), would have recognised my writing as related in any significant way to his own historicist and homo-erotic poetry. But what Cavafy and our own Lawrence Durrell would have appreciated was that Cheltenham in the 1960s had an authentic Alexandrian air of complacent decadence. The spa-town was still elegantly Regency but dilapidated, unrestored and gently louche.

I arrived there in an autumn when Mods and Rockers were rioting in the Promenade and there was a vainglorious rumour that the town was the Gay Capital of England. A dash of bumbling James Bond had been added to the suburbs by an ever-expanding Intelligence outpost of the Foreign Office.

My appointment had been that of a very minor Lecturer in English to a long-established, all-male teacher-training college. It was Low Church Evangelical, biased to physical education and housed in an Oxford College-style quad of roughly Gothic buildings, 1849, by Samuel Daukes, with a vast, grim Bodley-style chapel of 1909–10.

As a condition of appointment I had agreed, jokingly, to serve as Warden to the one hundred and seventy young men who lived in. Under my predecessor motorbikes had occasionally been driven along its top corridors so I was supposed to be popular but firm. There was, on the far side of the town, a sister college; and a very British tension, more moral than academic, existed between the twin establishments, which met only on Sundays in Chapel.

It was a position calculated to inflate my self-importance and I enjoyed every minute of it. At meals in Hall I presided from Top Table supported by ten student officers and any visiting guests. Several hundred young men had to wait to eat until I had tinkled a silver bell and said Grace. Then a second tinkle was needed before they could leave; so I had to eat with indigestive speed or cutlery would be rattled impatiently.

Teacher training colleges are always ranked well below real universities, but at that time, under an inspired and generous Principal, Edward Bradby, the place was enjoying a brief prime of experiment. Our genetic epistemology was streets ahead of that of Oxford and Cambridge colleges because we really cared about the mechanics of learning. The PE lads, who were the aristocrats of the student body, had been persuaded, against their image, to perform sinuous educational dance before the High Altar of the Chapel; and in the same dim venue the Combined Courses interpreted a painting, Duccio di Buoninsegna's *The Majesty* by a script and evocative plain-chant. There was a later experiment by the Religious Knowledge Department with live sheep in Chapel but that was rather less successful as sheep are wilful and there was a Wilton carpet.

It was a vibrant, exciting time, the best decade of a bad century when, thanks to the Beatles and the Stones, antique old England had most improbably become Earth's Capital of Trendy Youth. Birmingham, where much of our students' training practice took place, was still shivering from the memory of Enoch Powell's 'River of Blood' speech. Some of the excellent little secondary modern schools up there had been confused by a wave of immigration and we had sometimes to coax our men through complex, rewarding experiences in difficult classrooms.

One revelation in male fantasies was our Old Boys Weekend. Men relish rituals and require them. The Old Boys had loved the College for its formal oddity and when the Principal began his welcoming speech with 'Gentlemen', it was ritual to roar back 'We are!' and then cheer delightedly. All those ageing headmasters and senior teachers were returning to the scenes of their youthful repression and irresponsibility to assert themselves.

It was a hugely enjoyable time, when I made friends for life; and I remain grateful for the absurd, but creative, structural formality of it. Hence this poetic response to five Alexandrian years: a very English experience with Graeco-Egyptian undertones.

Cathedral meeting

In Cambridge thirty years ago
When ration books were regular
And Young Conservatives a rebellious, visionary youth,
I loved, with a repressed but absolute intent,
A handsome student, one year my junior.
Loved him so much I tried to join the Church
For two more years, thighs and theology.

All fell apart.
Half by the good sense of the man himself,
Half by the feeble wearing out of time.
He left for Africa and marriage to a clergy girl.
I went my own way on to find my lust
With less hypocrisy, but never lost
After that last tense Cambridge term
Our two-week cycling holiday in France:
Sun and no money,
Tents by the roadside verge
His strong bare legs by tent flaps standing tall
As I awoke at unwashed morning time.

And now, only by chance,
The news that he was back
And canon residentiary.
Four months I waited. Then this February day
Walked in the Midland city afternoon
And came at Evensong to see him pray.
The choirboys first, appraising-eyed,
The verger with his rod,
Last from the dog-arched shadows walked
My priest of God.
A heavy man of fifty, sweetly voiced and pendant jowled.

He settled in his corner stall of canopies and spires
Then, like a pilot, took control of organ, words and choirs.
Through the Magnificat and Simeon's prayer

I saw how rheumily those knees bent now
That tempted me in a cool Picard dawn.
And as a faithless Christian all the years,
When he'd been constant,
Have to say that I was moved.

After the service, half unsure,
Half playing with the incident,
I followed where the boys had filed
Into the cloisters by the chapter door.
And there he was.

'Hello,' I said, full of significance,
But was not recognised.
Seconds – his face faltered, then
'Not Brian Earnshaw!'
Should we have shaken hands?
For palm to palm is holy palmer's kiss.
We didn't anyway. I laughed.
We talked, each sensed the other out.
He found me wanting, so I let him go.
Old age it is
That crumbles almost lovers so.

After visiting Dyrham House to give my students period background for English 17th-century Literature

There was a student in my car
Coming back from the Field Trip to a house
Frozen by the National Trust
In mist and trees and a closed Cotswold valley.

He sat quietly in a back seat
While I still talked art.
When I asked him what he was doing, he said
'Trying to remember the team Swindon played in 1969'.

When you teach people Restoration Drama
And their real chance in life
Is almost professional football
They have a detachment Dryden can't penetrate.

He knew footballers well enough
In local clubs and shower rooms
To say that they cared for money and were indifferent to the game.
'I love being with them,' he said.

They might end up with a pub
Or a small town sports shop
But that was all right.
I don't know what he meant and he didn't care to tell me.

He was short and ginger haired,
Into punk rock and long sideburns.
His PE lecturers were nervous of his ability
And he considered me a literary amateur.

Such social confidence disturbs me,
So I asked about his parents.
It was all his father
Though he rarely saw him:

11

A large dark Scot, moved from the RAF
And driving a long-distance lorry in Europe,
Fluent in German, ignorant in French
But based in Paris and totally content.

One trip he'd gone with his dad
And found he lived in a red-light district.
'And your mother? Are they separated?'
'Only in fact; she gets along.'

Now next week, when it's Milton
And Satan with Sin and Death come to the gates of Hell
How do I know if his mind is with the second-hand word
Or the first-hand triumph of the soft green field?
Lectures don't matter all that much.

The Revd Dawson Bowling – Old 'Ten Pin'

The Chaplain died a little while ago
An old man I loved to argue with
And beat in public at top table.
A fat old man
Walked slowly down the kitchen corridor
And had the eye of death already on him.
Why did we argue so,
And score so viciously
Night after night at crowded tables?
I think because we both loved youth
And worked to make them listen to us,
And hated age
And so loved truth.

He brewed home wines
That gave me headaches
And in his basement,
I think against his wife's real wishes,
Three students lived
To talk to him at breakfast time.
And I was glad that when he died
Early one morning, crying out with pain
Because a heart that laughed would work no longer,
Only those students were beside him there
To lift him moaning down the stair
And ring the family
And do those practical things
That happen when you die in term time.

Inter-racial Poetry: March 1978

At a teacher training college
I tell a group of students
How I would teach poetry in schools,
Were I them.
The exercise is unreal in the case of two
For they are black Rhodesians
And I could never be them.
You'd think poetic method might
Leap two continents and one sea,
But no, apparently
They claim to feel contempt
Because I ignore their patriotic free verse
And am unaware of the rich literature
Of English-speaking Africa.

So the situation is set
And I have asked them to try their hand
At Poetry in Performance.
My own demonstration is modestly successful:
I give them each a line or so to read
And we create
A Sunday Street in Newcastle.

Now it is Selim's turn.
'I think we will have Mr Earnshaw to play the baboon.'
He smiles, and hands me a slip of paper
On which is written one word,
'Bakkoum'.
I have had richer roles.
But, desperate to show willing,
I nod, and frown at the paper.
'We will have you up here on the table,'

He continues.
And, since I stressed the need for dramatic movement,
I climb up nippily,
Except for that slight fumbling of middle-aged boots,
And squat there planning war
Since now I find that that's what poetry performing's for.

The others stand around and mouth their bits of paper:
'The dawn wind stirs in the bush'
'Rubbing branch against leaf'
'And light against darkness'
'High on his hill sits the baboon,'
Says Selim,
'Watching the night roll far from him;
And there he beats his chest and cries
" Bakkoum".'

Wordsworth has much to answer for.
The first reading was desultory,
But I pitched into my word
Boomed it out twice
And beat my chest to show that a monkey's part can be played
    trendily.
I saw Selim hesitate.
So made them work on its potential power again.
This time calling 'Bakkoum' several times as an inspired
    improvisation.
With more breast-beating and a smug sensation
Of being on top again
'Ideally,' I said, 'you should all group below me and look up,
Saying your lines to me
As the baboon Lord of the Mountain.'
The group crouched down
And did not disagree
So I moved on to safer subjects hastily.

Why Selim began this remains obscure.
In Africa his people fight
While he sits here secure
In western gardens where the airs are mild.
I suppose I'd feel uneasy too,
Sitting at the foot of Cecil Rhodes' effete grandchild.
Dangerous, however, to give me one word – 'Bakkoum'.
Since all of us, white or black
Are all too ready on the hot hills to squat
And play baboon.
'Bakkoum.'

Best way to go

Found a dead bee
In a November rose
Today.

At first seemed sleeping,
But I brushed him off
And he fell brittle
With the petals shedding.
The rose was blown.

Good end, I thought,
In a blown rose to die
Below the great clouds at the long year's ending.
And hope I do the same
In beech leaves, sunshine and a fall of rain
Sudden and sad and sharp with pain,
Clutching a cognisant regret
Never to wake again.

That flat in Parabola

I think it was the coldest night of the year
And a young man lying in the bed next to mine.
That near.
Wondering if I would try anything.
Good-looking man
Fair curly hair and brooding eyes
Inclined at certain watermarks of evenings plied with drink
To hint his recent army past was kinkier than you'd think.
He must have drunk too much
Because he got up twice to relieve himself.
And I lay there
But never said a word
Or precisely wanted to.

What cogs are slipping now, I wonder.
No young man here tonight
Just me considering
Why I grow tentative
To probable delight.
What was that line in Richard Three?
'I thank my God for my humility':
Most apt in minor register
For such a rogue as me.

Epithalamium

For a student president at a teacher training college, old style

Four hundred years ago Edmund Spenser
Lost his wife's wedding presents,
Or perhaps never really bought them;
Blamed it on the wild Irish
And wrote her a poem instead.
Now, with the happy couple here both taking Main English,
No-one would say he was wrong
To crown Holy Matrimony
With rhythm and song.
  So here we go.
On the day of the Rolling Stones' funeral party
On a day when a low-pressure area crossed the South briefly
Then left us high and sun born again,
Jeff Moule married Jackie Elton
To the pleasure of their friends
And the smiling cooperation of the Holy Trinity.

The Principal came and expressed a quiet satisfaction
That his little old chapel
Could still hold Jeff
Two weeks after the start of a dynamic presidency.
And Jeff
Who'd given his wife a ring of white gold
With 100-carat confidence
Admitted he felt kind of confined
Having to bend his neck a bit
Getting into the place,
But hoped to get a decent-sized cathedral
In time for the christening.

The Reverend Whales was certainly there
With his indefinably 1930-ish air.
But, in an atmosphere tense with creative English,
Caused some disappointment by not driving up the aisle
On his with-it motorbike

19

And P G Wodehouse smile.
As Jeff said:
'In a College of Education
we prepare to amuse the children of the nation,
and, as a sign that wedding preparations had been made,
I'd expected the Clergy to prepare at least one good visual aid.'

But the Reverend Whales had been married
Some years himself
And his patience was wearing thin.
So he blessed Jeff into silence
And announced the next hymn.

He didn't have to bless Jackie into silence
Because she's quiet already.
And that's where our chief hope lies in this marriage:
That Jeff's noisy descant
And her soft sub harmony
Will make sweet music together,
Well into the twenty-first century.
Bless them O Lord from Heaven your Dwelling Place
(Which must look very like a well-ordered classroom).
Bless them with years of good teaching
Patience, kindness
And the bright pleasures of their love.
May they always entertain their children with invention
And entertain each other in their dark cellar,
Bright-painted with Winnie the Pooh pictures.
And may this rampageous Innocence of Heart,
Sealed here at Midsummer
With friends round attending them,
Carry them always, lifelong and loud laughing,
Heavenwards at earth's ending.

A Warden's duties

One hundred young men in my nervous charge
Must lead their women out by half past ten.
Then I pace round five corridors
To check the end of loving when,
Sharp-eyed authority,
I pass each bedroom door
And drive my dominating heels
Into the wooden floor.

Always the Warden, keeper of the gate,
Earning my extra thousand pounds
Playing the man who's fun to hate;
And fantasise three students armed with axes
Marching before me, as in Fascist state,
Life can be fun, you know,
For me at any rate.

Take more than November to finish me

[a bit of tub-thumping]

Back to the world before I knew you
And the dark time before you came;
Autumn is muddy and indifferent,
Chrysanthemums smell much the same.
Only I change and only suffer
Because I knew too much delight,
Threw all I had to cross the Channel
And share a city for a night.
Only I change and see the difference:
A secondary road to joy,
Time has come in and chilled our loving
Time can do nothing but destroy.

I can do more than Time or Autumn;
I can make love and fight the years.
Don Quixote rides again this season
Greets the dull citizens and cynic cheers;
Off to a clash of rusting armour
And rotting leather at my knee.
I will tilt down the miles against us,
When you hear trumpets
Know it's me!

For here I come against discretion
Economy or common sense,
Doubtful at last of your reaction
Whether you value me or pence.
I only know that, if I falter
In my mad canter through your shires
There will be stillness and no singing
There will be cinders and no fires.
Pity me then in resolution,
Confused by all that just has been,
Hesitant standing at the station
Cry 'I am certain',

Intervene!
Kill that so steady long a limpness,
Tread down the unsaid might-be love,
Talk at my side and we will scatter
All the staid doubts you've made me have.

Hoping
Wet evening
Broken-stone pit-stack,
To the Black Country
I come back.

Riding so down on Upper Gornal
I will divide cold Reason's ranks:
Scrabble of hooves and clink of spurs
And ash trees brown on the colliery banks

And when I clatter down the lists,
Uncalled, unheralded, unsung,
And they ask why I trouble silence,
Say, 'he is ageing and still young.'
Be my excuse that I am lonely,
That I still need you in my bed.
The truth is that I must be faithful
When I deny us
I am dead.

A hot day, running by bus from Key West: August 1972

Across the aisle a veteran youth, moustached and empty from
    his war,
Is listening to a liberal queer who thinks his arse worth fighting
    for.
Through royal skies of small, sharp clouds the storms pass
    distant out at sea.
Wood balconies and jalousies and humid winds on Pigeon Key
To emphasise through endless space the heat-soft selfishness of
    me.

I need this thunder world that shows
Through Greyhound's tinted window sides.
Behind me, sitting in the bus, grey-haired, destructive, old and
    good
The hypocritic liberal rides.
A week ago this liberal fought outside Miami's barricade
And now, by gently devious lies, a legend of the left is made.
'And do you know
What really got me uptight was that
Though we had been completely open about our plans to
    demonstrate
The Police had parked this enormous barrier of buses between
    our boys and the
        Republican Convention hall.'

Thread drawn and sweet as Spanish limes my thoughts fall
    sickly from my head.
I speculate, in this blue heat, on an America gone red.
Long hippy hollowed out with hash
The veteran has a shell of sense.
'Don't nobody push me around,' he says, 'they hit me, I hit
    them.'
'Don't you like wrestling sometimes?' The liberal smiles gently,
'Wrestling with a friend?'
'Heck, friends don't wrestle with you! What sort of friend's
    that?'
The liberal sees the warning eyes, and cuts his answer flat:

'I remember this one line of French poetry. It goes,
Il pleut dans les, let me see,
Il pleut dans les rues, that's right, et il pleut dans mon coeur'.
'Are you French?' the veteran is helpful again.
'No, I'm Jewish.'

And I start guiltily as if I have invented the collusion
Of race and sex and politics to fascist fake confusion.
But it happened, and I write it.
And so survive, when vapouring is done
The easy truth that dreams of sex and dreams of heat and
    dreams of politics are one.
White herons and black pelicans
Excheque alone the weedy shore,
Patterned on shallow running tides
That slant the ocean floor.
Lost where in creeks of jewfish shades
I sleep my mental everglades.

In Worcester Royal Infirmary after a bad smash-up

Time for a silence
Now the hurrying hours
Stop for white ceilings
But no scent of flowers.
Strange to mourn absences
But flowers should be
The sharp accompaniment of injury.

I breathe once deeply and try fingering
That vacant hour of lost remembering:
Sunshine and movement upon melting snow
But nothing reaches where my mind should go.
Grieving at emptiness, hospitalised, I lie,
Knowing how simple it will be
At the next bend of road to die.

First rehearsal

Cream colonnades collected in November
A bright, wild day in Regent's Park
Where order ends
And zoos begin.

I went because a friend asked me
And at my age
The flattery is strong
To play Lord Byron in *Don Juan,*
Even to ropey back-street studios and schools
That have it set for A level.

The first-floor room where they rehearsed
Had golden palmettes fretted on the ceiling
And bunk-style beds by cluttered kitchen sinks.
The cast was young:
Two raunchy men who summed me sourly,
One pretty girl with water-curling hair
And a firm woman, desperately thin.
In fact they were all thin
And interested me
More than I interested them.

The men were leggy,
Coolly selective in the eyes,
Their jeans worn tight-to-genital the thighs.
One had a melancholy rake of nose,
Cheap silver on his fingers
And the mannered mime
That drama schools predictably design.
The other mattered more:
A lewd-eyed limber schoolboy
Chest hair twining up his throat,
Who might change his sexual nature
As often as his coat.

These two were fencing with a whip of foils
And wrestling when the sharp steel failed them.
Lean stomachs taut
As the checked shirts rucked up.

While the firm women made me tea
I sat there wondering, predatory,
What was in this for me?
I said, 'this cornice is pure Papworth
The motif's in his ironwork in Lansdowne Crescent.'
Then felt the air grow cold
With that slight, empty cleverness
Of knowing names and being old.
Yet, even as I spoke,
Felt the fresh touch of loins unknown,
Fingered the crisp exposé
Of pubic hair I'd never see
Emerging from tight clothes
The usual gap from age to youth.
My lust all fantasy and theirs some truth.

Aware of not belonging
I stood uneasily.
Then pitched into Byron's first line:
'I want a hero, an uncommon want.'

And probably I do
So still go looking
For heroes in the primal rite of fucking.

Should flowers be picked?

At Down Ampney
'A very noble seat
Situated with great convenience for pleasure and profitt'
Aubrey three hundred years ago
'Heard thirty milk mayds singing.'

Last Wednesday
To the 'meadowes on the west sides
Where departure a great number of cattle'
I went upon those whimsical excursions
That townsmen use to capsulate the land.
And heard no milk mayds.

Nor expected to

But walked with you
Unreasonably nervous to delight
Into those Lammas Fields,
The flat, reversed, green heavens of sluice and duct
And stream and conduit and becalmed canal.

Somewhere three hares boxed in the field
Or should have boxed.
I think most naturalists
Live like old Christians in some seeing hope.
But hares were there,
Lasciviously sociable
And one heron surly in reed beds.

We passed the cottage by the choked basin,
Where tub boats from Swindon
Waited on water freshets
In the high levels.
And there they were:
Last relict of alluvial common ground
And Saxon tenures,
The snake's head lilies.

You were spiteful.
I have to say this because it is interesting.
When rareness riots, it confuses joy;
And countless flowers of speckled purple
Or Easter white,
Active in winds and restless in deep grasses,
Drove you mad.

They do you know.
It is the trial of our times.
You wished I were not there
With you in willows early on the Thames.
It was a time you did not wish to share,
Lapped in damp hayfields and slow streams,
You wished I were not there.

Young Henry VIII writes to Katherine of Aragon as a Renaissance Prince

For you
I would do every matter that should please
Call Primatitch and Pollyoley here to paint
Immodest harlots on our plaster walls
Bring from Italy
Masters most marvellous for my Chapel choir.
I have brought stuffs from France,
Bought in one week
A thousand pearls
And lavished pounds
For prick-song to delight you.
What one man with a kingdom can –
I do.
But may not single-handed set up columns
Or take a chisel to some butter stone
And chop fat naked boys to pleasure you.
Give me a year
And I will make
Christendom shake, to hear of me.
We two shall have the suns of art to shine
And for us only.
Ah! there are organs on their way
Shall fill my house with music.
I only ask you wait.
I only ask you love me and be patient.

When you discipline students who are in love

I had a Christmas card yesterday
From two people I fined five pounds
For loving each other,
So that rates me a success
In human relations.
I caught them in the quadrangle,
Not love making,
Not even together.
Moonlight and voices under the stairs,
Feet hurrying,
Creeper leaves shaking
In the wild night
Mild night
Voices torn midnight;
Draught beer and soft milk-stout
And late-night parties flickering out.

He stood there on the lawn cursing me
And I laughed and jumped round him
Because I'm the Warden of the Residents
And Wardens fine people,
They don't have to take life seriously.
But he did.
So I dived under the rib vault of the stone porch,
Clicked on the hidden light:
Darkness of buttresses
Revelation of mistresses,
At least she didn't curse me.
'You've got to go home,' I said,
I was enjoying it but embarrassed,
And he swore again
Till I led them to the back door
And left them on College lawn
Pleasure and night-time torn,
Warden of the Residents
Walking the empty corridors,
Powerfully negative

To make up for being old.
Twenty minutes later
On a corner turned
Soft light burned
Stairhead,
I met him again
Upset him again
And we talked in the shadows like worldly men.
'What could I do?' I said.
'Let us both go to bed!'
'No,' I said
'No,' I said
'Not till your marriage lines are read
And then not in a College bed,'
And asked him why he hadn't seen her home
In the sharp night
Half light
Creeper-leaved moonlight.

He laughed then and left me
In disciplinary superiority,
Back to my room and sleep,
Leaving her there to creep
Up on the fire escape
Into his room and deep
Love him all college night
In his small college bed,
'No,' was what I had said.

All this long after learnt
Told why he paid five pound
With condescending sound,
And sent this card to me
Friendly and Christmasly,
Warden reflectively.

Not far from Spring, travelling to Birmingham

A black horse by a grey canal
And the dark trees' last festival.
Running, he was, to celebrate the light
As if this day were Plato's own
And Worcestershire were infinite.

What can I do to make you run,
To leave you animate and black?
Two years I fight
And still you are
Only alive when you make love
Or drive a car.

'Two years,' I think, 'must witness all,'
And Lickey Incline slows the train,
Back to attempt my Frankenstein
And play with corpses once again.

A mile above Alfoxden on English Field Week with twenty three awkward students

At England like a flooded field
Severn tentatively touched
And sun touched
Unexpectedly
In a wet Field Week,
Thunder showered and pulled
By personal crossness.

So I am here
Ten yards from everyone
Sat upon Quantock,
Haunted by Dorothy
William and Samuel
Who came up tramping
Sturdy from Hoddercombe
To eat beef sandwiches
Dry-lipped on Beaconhill.

Up here they came each day
In thick brown clothes,
Only a short way,
In the pale beech Spring
And Severn fingering the muddy shore,
From the last mistake
Which they
Like most of us make
Of not loving the right people
At the right time
Hard enough.

Grumpy with students
Who cut my path from side to side
When we walk,
As Coleridge did to Hazlitt
On Wem road
Shrewsbury-wards,

I see my same danger:
Not loving hard enough,
Not giving long enough,
Turning to Nature
Or a fat cat at suppertime.

Down now to Taunton Dean,
Crowcombe in the red valley,
Ruthless to pleasant things
Make love all summer.
Always remember
Life ends by not trying.
Not loving you
All those miles away
More than students, Field Week and old ladies with dogs
Is dying.

Going to Stratford to see David Warner's 'Hamlet'

To make love in a hired room
After a successful performance of Hamlet
Was a mistake;
Elizabethan rafters, a cistern siphoning,
The floorboards noisy
And the habit of analysing.
Night should have been left to sleep.
King, Queen, Prince, Councillor,
Trapped in a mad-hatter's tea party:
The chairs like coffins
And the table black.
Tearing England into unenchanted circles
Next day, you drove me back.

It made no difference
That a river of rain poured down Dinmore Hill
Or that the sun was warm at Ludlow,
You were always kindly,
Detached and suffering.
You have forgotten about other people.
Remain kind to them
And you need never remember.

I always wanted to play against candles
On a darkened stage
And offer excuses to Laertes.
Your hair in the darkness
Tumbled over the sheet tops
Pretending to be lovers,
But do you know that when I came to that climax
Shattered by your patience
I wasn't even thinking of you,
Only of someone in a park that morning.

Halberds marching in order
And tapestries,
Much better than car journeys.

When I wanted to see that Stuart church above the canal
I don't think you were very pleased
Because you couldn't help remembering for a moment
That I was human, with tastes and appetites,
Though little for the proofs of love
Sweated in hotel room nights.
'There lives within the very flame of love
A wick or snuff that will abate it.'
This is so.
Seven weeks and all that makes me burn
Will go.

It wasn't so much that you
Didn't want to come with me
As that you never realised
How many lies it takes
To launch a surreptitious love affair.
And if you love more than just lovers
Probably it's best to stay at home
With the television
And easy, tried relationships
Where you can grumble and burp
Without counting the effect of it.
Sensitivity is a bore
At the best of times,
And, when you're only half in love,
Becomes so more.

Don't you see that Hamlet is not necessary?
You can always live in the suburbs.

If you're still listening
There may be some point
And
Wait for it! This is a real scream!
Sex might not matter very much,
I only said might,
No intelligent person really makes his mind up
About killing an uncle
With all those gongs and cannon sounding

And black gates closing.
But Sex might be only a gentle curiosity.
After all you started it for just that reason
To see what I looked like
Naked on a carpet
And how I behaved.
You know now.
I'm a bumbling idiot.

But what really interests me
Is whether there's any love left
When the dynamic of exploration's exhausted.
I feel that there might be
But a car wasn't the place to find it.
I love this word 'might'.

In Paris
The last day there

I never saw you
All the cold morning.
But then I hardly expected to
Though the restaurant
Butted out into the pavement.

The mood in the Boul'Miche is suave this year;
The suits are charcoal, carefully striped in chalk,
Tout près du corps
To give people something to change to.
But one of the coats,
It was a pink one,
Had sixteen pockets
All with handkerchiefs.
I would like a body
With sixteen hearts
Dribbling affection
For you to cut out one by one
And take the sixteen hearts away.
That would leave none.

If I could shoot as high in my love making
As the fountain in the Luxembourg
Still I would never disturb the sailing boats
In the eight-sided pond of your affections.

Blanche of Castille,
Anne of Austria
Marguerite of Provence
All the dead Queens of France
Stand in the gravel walks.
Winter coming and the flat clock
Depressing the quarter hours
Of sunlight.
Here is the greatest wilderness of all
Not that you loved others

But that loving no one,
Chaste in a Paris autumn,
You would not love me.
All the dead Queens of France,
The salvias waiting for the first hard frost,
And the turned chestnut tree.

The National Assembly is pillared on the river quays
And on the hill behind
In melancholy gardens
The Senate meets in the Luxembourg.
Sing Senators
The weariness of love.
Most of my time was wasted time
And half of life is thrown away
All Souls' Day in the Père La Chaise,
Chrysanthemums for Baudelaire
And you indifferent studying,
Mere miles away.

I suppose there are gloomier places
Than the great town churches of Paris
Etienne, Sulpice, Gervase,
Down and outs snoring by holy water stoups
And a grey greatness
Weighing the spirit.
God had a long run in this unkind city;
Now
For all the new statues
And tricks of publicity
He hasn't got much longer.
And I'm just leaving.

After the Crooked House Inn

I post the letter in the day
Although I wrote it in the night.
Half of our day is night,
So to post darkness to you in the day
Though it is comfortless
Is right.

Give me an answer if you can
For I am old this time of year,
Drink Guinness in a Crooked House
Drive dirt roads in my roaring car
Hear mine streams pouring in the dark
By railway lines where no one goes
And see an end of loving near.

But loving never needs to end.
I roll the penny up the wall,
Step drunken in the twisted rooms,
Hear the sixth formers chat their girls
And know because you humour me
That I shall give
And you take
All.

Why should I lie to you in dusk
Or cheat myself at what I do?
All that I give goes like the sluice
Through bents and fennel into night
As nothing to my great return,
For what I gain from it is you.

There are subsidences in earth
Where shafts collapse and adits drain,
The hollow places of the mind
Where bitterness must remain.
Let me express myself in night
And live to love you without shame

To hold you through the tears I shed
And drive on main lit roads again.

For we shall meet in nothing else
But only on these roads at dark.
Here is our bed
Among old mines
And crooked houses and stale drink.
These parts must be our loving place
These fragments of dead time our link.

Early morning

Pisanello made medallions,
Long-nosed Florentines,
Bankers of Siena
And ladies whose dowries
Stuffed gold in carved cassones.

All this short summer night
You lay beside me
Pulling the bedclothes
Firmly to cover you.
And I, who turned crotcheted on my twisted shoulder
Holding a little of clothes to cover up nakedness,
Looked at you sometimes
Lying with your back to me
Never to face to me,
Calm in the eighth light night,
Quiet in starling-calling morning
And milk floats jingling.

Botticelli painted satyrs
Asleep, puzzled in exhausted lust;
Called high-breasted women from the green woods of the id
Who will never return there
But stand
Smiling and confident
Upon my hearth rug,
Or lie in the still earliness of day,
Possessive among my tumbled sheets,
Bewildering me
With slim thighs,
And long arms shadowing me.

Climax of time,
You are gone now,
And I sit before coffee
Keeping you in my mind
With bronze medals and green tempera,

Shut from all images of life or voices talking.
Come very seldom to me Love
Night time and morning
Flowers in long fingers, feet in grass
And day birds calling.

Last day of the year and the holiday

Too many sunsets on too many roads
Of mistletoe and temperament and towns.
I have sat by you till our souls were bare
And picked our private persons clean
Of every pubic hair.
And still I love you in a ruined style
And hate the dark tree flowing of the Marne
Silo and water tower
And winter cloud
That brings the Paris evening leaving you
Nearer with every mile.

So you can scratch between my legs next time
Chew down my finger nail,
(first finger on the left hand)
You know the minutes of my every itch,
How soon the best cathedrals bear me down,
When I will pull in to relieve myself,
What pintables and which
O which sad scrapings of our mutual scurf
Worry us down
And undermine
Our actual worth.

Endless memorials to un-needed wars
Fought for the emptiness of all this France,
The rear lights level
And the sunset too,
Chasing an M.G. Midget through the Aisne
I sit here next to you.

I have a recipe for all despair.
Count the long poplars and the spindle trees,
Drive helpless, hopeless, raging with you
Europe everywhere.

Chastleton House

House in a high wind
Open to dust
And sunshine,
Patterned so much with years
That just to enter through the garden door
Was to be full of shadows.
You drove away from the enlightened country,
The trees bottled with age
And the dovecot by the cattle well.
Drove into sunshine
And I chose shadows,
So much better than you.
I hope the ice cream was satisfactory
And the gesture made up your ego.
Me, I grow tired of building other people,
Tired of Jacobean play rooms that only I see.
Sometimes I will have company
And you will be satisfied with sunshine.
Sometime I will find a compromise
Of age and affections
And someone to enjoy with me
The hobby horse for seven children
The pomegranates and the plaster work.
I wonder who it will be
In another Spring
And another house
In high windy country.

Very late November

Chaucer says:
'A thousand tymes I have heard it tell
That there is joy in heaven and pain in hell',
And heard it wrong.

The letter never came today.
You left me to my usual work:
Viscounts in Mercedes
Moving smoothly through the Bois de Boulogne
To weekend hideouts on the southern Seine,
Smoothly with you,
Golden-haired and compliant,
Always a sucker for sophistication.
I grow old fast at this time of year.

So I walked through suburbs to The Folley
For the discord of a rugby match.
We were beating Reading University
Rather easily,
The girl friends pinched at the touchline,
The Cotswolds drab across the willow fields;
And I suppose that for an hour
I forgot.
But if, some winter afternoon,
I ever do forget,
That will be the end of me.
Because the reason I am here alive
Is that I care,
And breath a purpose from this suffering air.

Mid February

I live within white Gothick doors
And lecture in a cave of ice,
Civil and kind they are to me
Students and casual studentry,
They drink my coffee half the night
And make my discontentedness and loss
More light.

Faustus
In such another place
Kept flattering half friends at his door;
I know they are no use to me
But echoes in this winter wood
Of what I had from you before.

And you are gone
And time corrupt
Has aged what we expect from time.
I take my exercise in town
And grope at what I hoped to be,
Money has settled on my mind
And spoils your exact memory.

We made love once
In a hotel at Sens
On the cathedral square,
Not much of love of course for you
But tolerant to let me do
After long absence what I wanted to.
You smiled, I know, and urged me on,
And turned and slept
When I was done.

But that was on some nebulae
Spiral and lost in your dark sky.
Besides,
Since this you have forgot
The purposes of what we were.
And I have not.

A possessive insanity that I want to keep

Dark miles after Ravenna
There was that Communist café:
The graceless drink in
Walk in
Drunken old man and shabby room
To talk in.
Filled you with white wine,
Sottish and small
And kissed you on the lips
When I had turned to go.
After these months a sharpness still mounts in me
With that old man
Because I hate him so.

Much better not

Make love would you?
Nothing so simple
On a drunken bed,
But weigh it in your next untooth-brushed morning
And find that love
Has all gone light
And dead.

There are these barriers
That stand in friendship
You must not climb,
However strong the beer.
Venture just once on the disordered senses,
Wind from the harbour blows,
You'll not return,
All round
The cliffs of love are sheer.

[To my mother]

Written in the car, outside Brough Castle

Most happy traveller, I hope you journey on.
Though seeing you there, lying on your back,
Pinch nosed and disapproving because I came too late,
I have my doubts.
For all that three-hour drive at night
Rarely at less than seventy,
Too late to rescue you from hospitals.

Good traveller, please, somewhere on
Highroads of Heaven, homely with tea-time stops
Wait for me patiently.

After a day taking students around architecture and paintings

I've done it
You know,
I've managed it again:
Walked all day in Oxford
With cheerful live people
And ended in a lonely evening.

I'd meant
For years
To see Uccello's picture once again:
Hunting by night
When the resounding horn should fright the satyrs from the
    hollows
And prepare
The empty glades to pleasure me
With open innocence
And calm suggestions of a revel field.
But when I climbed the stairs at the Ashmolean
It wasn't night
Inside the wood
And loutish boys on frightened horses
Chased five stags
On crooked courses.
Which was the end of an idea.

Then people weren't eager to talk to me afterwards
Because they were married
And television was less bother.
So I've fallen here
Very near
Cold-hearted hopelessness
About life's heartlessness.

What do you do I wonder?
There on the hill.
Cooking your complicated meals
And making love
One night a week
With cold dexterity
To the doctor's orders.

New Street Station

Seeing the two of them
Kissing on the platform
Not knowing
My looking,
Makes me wonder
How often what I do is seen.
You think you love in secret
And the world sits back on padded cushions
Watching curiously.

No lovers and no problems

At Summer term's end
There are bad dreams in College.
In the upper corridors
Comes and goes,
Missing a night
And random upon rooms of sleeping students,
A vampire nightmare of the early morning.

One woke to see a presence by his bed,
Sharp-toothed from horror comics,
That faded in the partly dark.
And some hear breathing
In empty corners.
Each in his separate sensual room they sleep
High in the roofs
And wonder what disturbs them.
I will not see or hear the formless ones
Because my dreams are wakening.
My world grows older than the things they see,
And tired of dreaming.

One of the students woke three nights ago
To so much fearing
That he left his bed
And switched the light on to expose what breathed
And leaned above him in the darkened room.
The bulb was dead.
He stood beside the wall
And the sound passed and there was nothing there
But curtains stirring with the hand
Of listless morning air.

Lights don't go on you know,
They never do.
The sexual phantoms of the night
Are not surprised by sudden light.
They fade,

And let you tell your friends next day
What spirit haunts you
And in what sly way.

So I have none
And I sleep all alone;
My corridors are silent till the cleaners come;
My walls are stone.

Black Wednesday, going back home

Bragg Lane and Fourscore Street
And plump-faced Pakistani girls
With chiffon trousers round their feet.
Better, I suppose, than you.
At least they wanted to be led
Past cross-grained white girls offering them a fight.
All that you met me for
In the sand-blast wind at Tipton
Was to stop me coming for the night.

And so you managed it
And I kill time
Waiting for trains, senselessly fond
Fixed by tomorrows
And Spring beyond.

But just this once,
Now that you're caught, hand to your mouth
In sheer bad conduct,
A favour for the next time!
Turn in the early morning when I touch
And sweat affection in a waiting arm,
Ask me to visit you when money's out
Advantage quite invisible;
Put me in doubt
What our mote-eyed, mud-trampled
Both sides self-mutilating
Love affair's
About.

Tuesday in teaching practice

Almost past repair today
And not really sure that I care today either.
After all, I have a road licence
And can scoot dangerously through the country
Of the upper Thames flooded,
In blue sky and elm trees
And open light.
And I have other friends,
Gestures against loneliness.

Just how do you do without me?
No, let's not take it that way.
The regret is mutual,
The liking was possible.
Only the messy tangle of limbs in darkness,
The surprise when the light went on,
Are quite unsuited to the fast roads,
The charming pop music
And the light about Fairford.

Please, in the shallow water of February,
Let seriousness come in again
With the barometer falling.
I want life to be dreadful
With responsibility
And the appalling burden
Of coping with your kind of quality.

A bad night four weeks away from you

Have you ever thought of the price that I pay,
Middle-aged man
Falling in love with the young?
Talking to you here
Time has caught up with me
Cruel in contrast
That wrinkles are for ever;
That the two at my neck
And the bar down my forehead
Will only fade when the bone that they cover
Breaks from its hiding place
In the last resting place.
Rest is for ever.
Here in the night of resounding unhappiness
Brooding on age and the skull's everlastingness
Think of me northwards
Fighting ahead of you
Sixteen years dead of you
Sometimes to write to me
Light to me
Sight to me
Ink and be bright to me,
Dark summer weather.

What happens when you try to stay alive

Short silence on a Sunday night
Trumpets still sounding
Out of sight.
'Nine times in love,' I told myself
And heard the sermon to the end,
Nine times in love, and middle age
Looks from my mirror with a winning smile
Ingratiating
And quite vile.
Rain in the air and voices going
To grey-green evening at the end of June.
Term ending
Love leaving.

Some years ago
I have been happily in love,
But that was in another climate
And still morning.
Here in this town
Salvation Army bands play in the promenade
To rockers lounging,
Lime trees flower in an older air.
Constancy is a mildewed word
'And you may love'
He tells me
'But you may not care.'
Short silence on a summer night
And this old town
And these wet roofs.
Gather myself to be urbane,
To be in love without disturbance
Laugh in the crowded swimming pool
And still feel pain.

Cimex Lectularius and us

Bed bugs aren't common now are they?
So infestations of them
In flat dead armies as we went to bed,
Dusted in pyrethrum powder,
Forgotten in love making,
Must make a hazard
Unusual to the affectionate.

You never know what the neighbours are like
Until the floor boards gape
The mattress teems
And your eye grows quick to movement in corners;
And I never know,
Though I grow
Notably older,
How young in infestation,
Caught here and there by sudden weaknesses
Of absolute liking,
I am
To you,
Until you talk seriously in the cool morning
Of where they live
And where they come from
And what,
Angrily involved,
You should be doing about the blood-brown bodies.

Only then,
Kneeling upon the dangerous sheets,
Set into contrast
Of the absolute in unromatic,
I realise what you never accept
In the warm dark bed
Or the record-loud morning:
You,
More than anybody,
You,

To the exclusion of memory,
Direct my middle years,
My early, middle and late heart,
And there is nothing,
Not pyrethrum
Absences
Or the cold analysis of joy
Can presently be done about it.

Somewhere there ought to be
Some way to be less vulnerable.
And there probably is
But only frightened people
Would need to look for it.

And I'm not very frightened.

Out of petrol in Cranham

I think Spring ended in the car last night
In a dark unbelief at what I do.
You have the wholeness of two-sided love
And find
That what you thought in the sheet-tangled time
Was of the moment
And,
Put under stress,
Untrue.

So subtle prostitution of our hands
Which met a while
But never meant to hold.
Two people in a surplus of old love,
Toiled by damp evenings
And the stress of friends,
Run out of petrol in the village hollow
And reach a point where faithful waiting ends.

You never know where the warped heart is bending
Or where the wash of flooded feeling goes
But treachery is in the woods this evening
And like this mist
My rank self interest rose.

This is why Spring has ended half way through
And this is what
In mental rot
My time of life will do.